Tacenda Literary Magazine

Fall 2012 Edition

Editor-In-Chief
Zoé Orfanos

Consulting Editor
Robert Johnson

Associate Editors
Felicia Afuan & Hanaleah Hoberman

Cover Design
Liz Calka & Carla Mavaddat

Text Design
Sonia Tabriz & Justin Song

BleakHouse Publishing
2012

BleakHouse Publishing
NEC Box 67
New England College
Henniker, New Hampshire 03242
www.BleakHousePublishing.com

ISBN: 978 -0-9837769-2-5

Printed in the United States of America

A Note From the Editor

TACENDA: n., pronounced ta'KEN'da – 'things better left unsaid'

Welcome to the most recent edition of *Tacenda Literary Magazine*. For years, *Tacenda* has filled its pages with the dynamic and often anguished words from the front lines of crime and punishment. The entire BleakHouse family proudly amplifies voices that otherwise might be lost. However, *Tacenda* accomplishes far more than publishing works that express the complex and bitter world of social justice. *Tacenda* provides a literary window into a prison cell, into a second chance at life, and into a warzone. In short, *Tacenda* provides and shapes literature.

Working with this press has redefined my idea of "literature." Rather than a book assigned by a professor, or carefully shelved in the library, literature arises from the words and ideas of regular people. The 2012 Edition of *Tacenda Literary Magazine* proudly showcases nine of these exemplary people. These authors have thoughtfully crafted and edited their stories to create fifteen crucial windows into crime and punishment. The issue begins with a reflective look at the meaning of "life" by Michael Ballard. Mr. Ballard offers a view of everyday life seen through the excruciatingly small lens of prison life. In a series of well-chosen details, he develops the idea of "life" into a living death.

Kimberly Meyer and Meghan Fort both offer a trio of poems to *Tacenda*. Ms. Meyer's short but powerful works span a wide range of topics including the bare reality of life in a women's prison and the crippling nature of enhancements on prison sentences. Meghan Fort brings the themes of social justice into barren, war-torn terrain. Ms. Fort strikes a careful balance between both sides of a consuming conflict.

Jordyn Cahill's essay "Frozen" presents a chilling window intro drug addiction and ruptured family life. Ms. Cahill finishes the issue with her poem "The Ones I'll Leave Behind." Her simple poem manages to give insight into countless facets of prison life including loneliness, anger, longing, and heartbreak. A beautiful poem about her father, Carla Mavaddat's "Baba" uses rich imagery to paint a portrait of her father. The magical, wistful tone of the poem is brought to bear wonderfully by Ms. Mavaddat's delicate voice.

William Roth, Andrea Robertson, and Amos Wright explore alienation and loneliness through three short stories. William Roth's visceral short story, "The Farmhand," centers on Homer, a rural teenager excluded from the local community for his slow demeanor. Hurt in his isolation, Homer complicates the idea f a tragic hero when he takes out his aggression on a young girl in the community. In the same vein, Andrea Robertson's "The Witch of Endor" explores the life of Cass Bergeron, a shunned and lonely psychic in a small town. Amos Wright relates the story of Larson, a man reentering society after being convicted of raping his daughter.

Finally we have Adi Stein's adaptation of the short story "The Crying Wall." Mr. Stein's prose-to-play adaptation stages an otherworldly scene in an otherwise ordinary prison. As an old man shows a younger prisoner the history and blood behind the walls of the prison, Mr. Stein invites readers to peer beneath the exterior and find the vital, pulsing core. Like "The Crying Wall," each piece of *Tacenda*'s 2012 issue forms another window into the heart of crime and punishment.

Zoé Orfanos
Editor-in-Chief, *Tacenda Literary Magazine*

Table of Contents

Life	Michael Ballard	1
Cell Block 6	Kimberly Meyer	3
Twelve Thur-tee	Kimberly Meyer	4
Frozen	Jordyn Cahill	5
Baba	Carla Mavaddat	9
The Farmhand	William Roth	10
Taking Action	Meghan Fort	26
A Hidden World	Meghan Fort	27
The Witch of Endor	Andrea Robertson	28
Enhancement	Kimberly Meyer	39
The Song of the Abyss Eater	Amos Wright	40
Subhuman	Meghan Fort	52
The Crying Wall *Short Story by Victor Hassine, Adapted for the Stage*	Adi Stein	53
The Ones I'll Leave Behind	Jordyn Cahill	58
About the Editors and Contributors		59

LIFE

Michael Ballard

Think of your favorite season of the year. Picture it. What activities do you while away your time with? For me, it's summer. I'm a summer-time kind of guy. Those days when it's warm, even at daybreak. And swimming: one of my favorite summer activities, running down to this great spot on the bank of the Lehigh. The place where there's an old rope swing tied to a Birch tree. Or packing up with the family and going to the shore. My boogie-board's tether attached to my wrist, gliding along the barrel as a wave built, crested, and washed away. Only to repeat it in the churning white-wash of the shallows.

Now think of an important event in your life. One that wasn't solely yours, one that you have an intimate connection to. If you're a parent, you've got a treasure trove of these. So pick one that stands out. My pick would be my childrens' weddings. The love, hopes, and dreams you feel and share with them on that day. Priceless.

Now, think of a milestone in your own life. Paying off the house. Paying for your child's education. Seeing your children grow up to be responsible, caring adults. Or just managing to remain employed long enough to provide for your family. Choosing a profession that affords you some measure of security at retirement.

Now imagine your only connection to these emotions and events is as a spectator.

Gone are the special moments a free person experiences without realizing what they mean. Gone are the times you hold your children. Gone are the celebrations at holidays, where you're surrounded by family and friends. Gone are the days of coming home to a family that loves you. Gone is your daughter's first dance recital. Gone is your son's first haircut. Gone are those moments you see your daughter go to her prom looking like a princess. Gone are those graduations. Gone are the phone calls asking for advice. Gone are the weddings. Gone is the announcement that you'll be grandparent. Gone is the joy of holding your first grandchild. Gone are those times you can enjoy the freedom of a ride on a motorcycle. Gone is the ability to choose your next meal. Gone are those days you can go fishing. Gone are the nights when you go out to dinner and see a movie. Gone is the opportunity to have a pet. Gone is every chance you'll have of ever creating or enjoying a meaningful memory—replaced by a fenced in compound where *life* exists, just outside the razor wire.

> Death: the act of dying, or state of being dead. ("Webster's New Pocket Dictionary" 2007 Houghton Mifflin Harcourt)

A life sentence is an emotional death. A life sentence is the removal of every emotional experience that "life" contains. Surrounded by other prisoners, most of whom you will see leave to go back to their families, their friends, and their communities. You're not even able to make a friend without knowing that that friendship is temporary. Daily—in fact three times a day—the permanence of a life sentence confronts you as the staff change shifts. Television displays facets of free life you can only feel fondly reminiscent of, facets that you will never again experience. Self-hatred and regret accompany each new day because you have only yourself and your actions to blame.

A life sentence isn't just an emotional death. It's physical isolation as well. Gone are the days of hugging another human being. You're an alien surrounded by strangers. Gone are the instances of holding hands or cuddling close to watch a movie. The ecstasy of sexual intimacy with someone you love, gone. Those desires unrequited. Human contact is replaced by cold concrete and steel.

Life in a Pennsylvania prison is lifeless. The permanence of these conditions is without question. Life in Pennsylvania is just that, a LIFETIME.

Cell Block 6

Kimberly Meyer

In a women's prison,
friendships form,
strangers relate,
grandmas cry,
mothers scream,
daughters fight –
just like outside.

In a women's prison,
colored pencils are worn
like makeup,
bunks are lived in
like houses, morning kisses come
from cell mates.

Prisoners ecstatic
to leave Block 6
come right back,
two
weeks
later.

Twelve Thur-tee

Kimberly Meyer

Why are you here?

I got a pass.

The doctor isn't in.

Well they signed my pass.
I got a pass.

The doctor won't be in
for an hour more.

I wanna wait.
That's why
they signed my pass.

The doctor isn't in.

I wanna wait.
They signed my pass.
He ain't comin'?

No, not yet.
The doctor won't
be in until twelve
thur-tee.
Twelve
thur-tee.

I'll wait, I got…

A pass, I know.

Time.
And no,
you don't.

FROZEN

Jordyn Cahill

I'm in the frozen water and completely panic-stricken. My cheeks are burning from holding the last bit of air within them. In my young mind, I already know what will happen the minute that I release the death-grip of my lips: I will lose my breath of air, the water will flood in and my small lungs will burst. This knowledge, and the chlorine burning my searching eyes, has increased my panic.

I don't know how I came to be in the frozen pool with my brother, but here we are—both of us struggling to keep our small mouths closed tight. Keep the air in. Keep the water out. I can still feel the ice above us, paneled along the top of the water. It lies as hard and cruel as cement above the pool. It taunts me. I can see the pool's ledge but my tiny hands cannot budge the ice's weight to reach for safety. The cracks along the ice's surface gives me hope for a hole, and just as I think we may get out alive, I see my brother on the pool's ledge. I do not know how he made it out when I did not. I cannot see the small spot on the ice that has saved him and bound me to my death. Now, along with panic, straining cheeks, and burning eyes, I am saddened and alone. I give up and sink, overcome with weight. Further, further, further, down I go until I am gone completely, watching him look at me from safety's edge.

That was my first true nightmare. I am sure that I also had the typical monster chasing, hurting, and haunting the dreams of every child's slumber. But no, this was my first *real* nightmare because it was possible. It existed in a reality I was close to: I had a brother, there were swimming pools in my life, and ice lay frozen on the tops of water in the winter. It did not matter that we lived in Central Florida and I had never actually seen a frozen pool. I knew they existed, and I knew that ice would kill me if given a chance.

For years I have thought of that dream, each time for very different reasons. I believe we are all given insight into life, whether we choose to accept it or not. I was around seven or eight when I had that dream, and what I could not have known all those years ago was that my brother and I would remain trapped together, bound in insane and profound ways. Our current stations in life display an undeniable relevance to the dream. But maybe I have it all wrong, and it was actually I who was freed and he who was left to suffer. Maybe my death was really life reborn, and his escape was a sentence all his own: watching me sink to the depths knowing he could not save me. A boy left at the edge of a frozen tomb where his little sister lay. That cannot be freedom.

I struggle with my feelings for my brother. Though I have spoken openly about it in support groups, I am still in the process of scouring the filth, shame, and confusion from its surface. How can a little girl love the brother who stalks her doorway at night? "You are my best friend. My confidant. How can you haunt me in the darkness? How can you fill me with black rage and razor-sharp void? Can't we just go back to what once was? Back before the pain? Please?" But we do not go back. It continues, and I continue to pretend to sleep soundly as it happens and I never confront him with the questions that weigh like hot lead on my little heart.

Maybe as a child I knew instinctively that we were both pained. Unless a person is a sociopath, does he not feel bad when he hurts others? Does he not have guilt or remorse? I knew he was pained, as I was. But I knew somewhere deep inside that he could not, or would not, control his hunger. I would always be the object of his pain. It was glue, not water in my dream. A glue stronger than any substance known to man. One that binds souls and destinies, the way the earth is bound to its axis. Maybe the ice was solidified sadness. A sadness so great it must be shared between two people because the sheer magnitude would crush just one.

I tried desperately to fill the void with sin, vice, or any desire that I could muster. Nothing ever worked. When I thought I was making headway, filling almost to the top, the bottom would fall out. I would try to stuff it again and again, to no avail. My pain only increased and expanded the perimeters of the void; and with every sin, vice, and desire, I stuffed more and more and more. I watched through pained eyes as my brother did the same thing. His pain, though so unlike my own, was enough for him to choose the same rocky and treacherous paths that I had. Or maybe it was I emulating his paths out of desire to remain bonded to him in a way that didn't hurt us as much. Maybe if I could focus on the joint we smoked, and try hard to hold that moment of solidarity tightly, it would hurt much less when his focus was later turned to me.

The tearing, searing, gnawing, shredding pain I felt helped to fuel my addition. I was dried grass, withered and sun-scorched, and my aching need to fill the void was too much to bear. My pain was the accelerant and my addiction the blue flame that ignited me. Soon I was engulfed and burning, and instead of pain ending, it flared and spread to all that I loved.

Of the drugs and substances I tried, none of them did for me what the majesty of painkillers could do. I chose the things I thought would soothe me. "Lull me to sleep, little darlings. Give me wings and set me free." Those deceptive little bastards only lied to me and betrayed the trust I had instilled in them. The pain would diminish only long enough for me to be aware that it was never really going to go away. I wanted to feel normal, and I sought normalcy through the abnormal channels of destruction and demise. The addiction that my brother and I shared, miles apart, was fueled by a pain so kindred that it bled.

Many years have passed and our lives—so similar for so long—are vastly different now. I am in prison and he is free to live with his wife and daughter. I am in prison and he has the freedom to relapse. I am in prison and he has the freedom to have a mental breakdown; to be held within mental institutions where he is diagnosed, monitored and observed. I am in prison. But I am sober, of sound mind, spiritually in-tune, emotionally aware, and cognizant. I am in prison, but so is he. His prison is flesh, his aching thoughts, his shameful past, and his inability to control the things killing him. I am in prison and will be released; he may never be.

If the dream were his, the pain of knowing that he escaped and I suffered may have killed him emotionally. Maybe it *was* his dream. Maybe he is now punishing himself for leaving me, trapped, under the ice of my own pain. Maybe his sentence is an unconscious, slow and methodical suicide.

I love my brother and I have forgiven him. I have expressed an all-encompassing forgiveness to him for everything. My dream has relevance I cannot fully comprehend. I still wonder how we got into that pool. For a long time I thought we fell. Now I think maybe he pushed me, as siblings do, and then realized his error when I sunk beneath the ice. Maybe he tumbled in after me to save me, but gave up the struggle when it was too difficult.

There are certain things I will never know. What I do know, however, is that it is now *I* who am helping to save *him*. I have fortified my resolve with love. I have fought through an addiction, cold as ice, and have found recovery. It is with that recovery that I extend the hand to him. I may have stayed trapped beneath the ice, but his freedom has left him frozen.

Baba

Carla Mavaddat

Cirque du Soleil's headless man
Printed meticulously several times on your dark blue tie.
A light purple shirt guarded by your navy suit,
Matched perfectly with your handsome smile.

You walked long, quick strides,
As you swung your briefcase back and forth.
You swiveled your way into the metro ready to depart,
And the magic began once you met your Italian friend.

Red and shiny, standing out among the many wheels,
Majestically and impatiently waiting for a speedy spin,
The Vespa zipped through the rush-hour streets,
Into a little alley where your arrival was announced.

Three hundred and sixty five days,
A year of silence and emptiness.
Where is he, with the twinkling eyes?

THE FARMHAND

William Roth

Homer drained the bottle and wiped his mouth. He wiped his small mouth, crowded by fat cheeks; his lips cracked from too much sun and puckered as though he were constantly ready to suck on his thumb. "They tore my shirt! They tore the sleeve right off!" Rocking back and forth on his feet he began to cry, moaning so deeply that the sound was almost inaudible. "They should'na done that. They should'na tore my shirt."

Suddenly, Homer stopped crying. Cramming his hand down into the chest pocket of his denim coveralls he searched frantically with his fingers. "And she kept my twenty-three bucks! She can't do that! She didn't give me nothing for it. She can't keep it! That ain't right!"

He tried to drink again, but the pint bottle was empty. With a half-grunt, half-sob he flung it into the darkness of the cornfield to rattle down through leaves, thudding softly against the broken earth. "Damn!" As he stumbled off the road, the overweight farmhand shoved through the shadowy rows of reaching black streamers; the more he thrashed, the louder they rattled mockingly. "Gonna find that bottle. Gonna find it and break it! Gonna break it good! Where is the damn thing? Where are you?"

His foot hit the bottle, sent it skittering away to clang dully against a stone. Springing forward, he trapped the pale shadow of glass in a prison of fat, sweaty thighs and arms. "Wouldn't break, would ya! Wouldn't give me what I paid for! Well, now Homer's got you again. This time I'm gonna smash you good! I'm gonna smash you into a million pieces! See how much ya like that!"

Scuttling clumsily back to the middle of the road, he lifted the bottle over his head, slammed it down to shatter against the asphalt, glass fragments spraying against his pant legs. "Make fun of me, will ya! Well, I guess I showed ya! I showed ya good!" Tears ran down his cheeks as he tried to get control of himself, tried not to cry anymore. He hadn't done nothin' wrong. They couldn't treat him that way. He hadn't done nothin' wrong!

Leaning against the trunk of a tree at the side of the road, the farmhand wiped his eyes with the back of his hand. His breath came harshly, making a whistling sound. He tried to stop the sound by closing his mouth, but couldn't keep his lips together. Homer shook his head wearily. His body was fat and sloppy. He hated it. Picking up a piece of slate, he scratched into the flesh of his bare under-arm with the point, scratched hard, so hard that it hurt even through his drunkenness. A small line of black appeared and began widening against the pale skin. Dropping the slate, he stared fascinated at the ragged thread of blood as though he didn't understand what it was, before yanking the red patterned bandana out of his hip pocket to scrub frantically at the wound. "They wanted to kill me! They wanted to beat me to death! And they would'a too, if the city girls hadn't been there, if Mr. Taney hadn't stopped 'em." Homer shook his head hard, agreeing with himself.

Then he turned to stare blearily back toward the faint yellow glow of Mooresville's night-lights squatting over the treetops. He whispered it this time. "They wanted to kill me…But I'll get 'em. Especially that Mr. Johnston. I'll kill Mr. Johnston." Grimacing, he inhaled sharply, wondering suddenly if once you said something like that out loud, did you have to do it?

Frowning, Homer shook his head again. He didn't care. He meant it. After peering carefully around to see if anyone was coming, he forced himself to repeat, "I'll get 'em." He punched his forehead with his fists. Not loud enough. Standing straighter, he spread his feet, clenched both fists digging his nails into his palms. After taking a deep breath, the farmhand shouted slowly into the darkness, "I will kill them all! I will make them suffer the way they made me suffer!"

Quickly he glanced up and down the road again. Even when nobody was coming, saying it scared him. Then Homer wiped his nose with the back of his hand. Anyway, he'd never do something like that. Just noise, that's all he was making. No way he was going to kill anybody. Pressing his fists into his eyes, the farmhand tried to stop crying. "But I didn't do nothing wrong! I just tried to relax, to be myself, like Mr. Taney had told me to." Homer snorted. "Just tried to be my fat, ugly self…"

The workers from the other farms had been late. Homer stood fidgeting with his pint of whiskey. He had bought his own this week. It was cheaper that way. He would buy two beers tonight, so Mr. Taney wouldn't throw him out of the bar. But he had brought his own whiskey, and had already drunk a little, though that was enough for now, no more. He didn't want to get sloppy.

Homer again went over in his mind the things he was going to say. Sliding the bottle into the back pocket of his coveralls, he practiced silently how he would recite the funny things he had memorized, where he would pause, which words he would say loudly so the others would get it. If he did real good, if he made people laugh he might get away with slapping somebody on the back, like the others did. Or maybe somebody would say, "You know, Homer, you aren't such a bad fellow."

The farm hand looked toward the door again. Where were they? It had been almost a half hour since he arrived, and no one else had showed up yet. "Where are the men, Mr. Taney?"

The crippled, bald bartender raised his head to squint from the street end of the bar where he was washing glasses, then continued his work without answering.

Shuffling toward the door, Homer stared down at the worn, stained linoleum floor as he passed where Mr. Taney stood so as not to be a bother. Stepping out onto the porch, out into the crisp, golden dusk of autumn farm country, the tall, overweight eighteen-year-old immediately saw the others gathered up the street in front of Mr. Butz's convenience store. Some squatted in a small circle; some leaned against the porch rail or moved about slowly. Homer could hear little edges of laughter crackling through the group and realized something special must be going on. Three men came out of the store door and sat down on the broad front porch step. Others yelled at them and laughed.

Harvest season, that was it. The potatoes would be ready next week. The farm hands made extra money helping bring in other people's crops once they finished their own. Homer's boss, Mr. Oswald, always hired three or four. The men were looking around to see what they might want to buy with the extra money. He shook his head. He had forgotten, but it didn't matter. He didn't plan to spend much of the money he had made, not on store-bought goods at least. Patting his chest-pouch pocket, he smiled slyly. He was saving his money for something else, for something special. Homer looked up the street again. Except that the other hands were together at the store now, obviously enjoying each other's company. If he hurried up the street he might be able to join them, to tell one of his jokes memorized from the mail order book.

Two more men came out of the store; then everybody began walking slowly down the sidewalk. Homer hurried back inside, "They're coming now, Mr. Taney! They was at Butz's store lookin' at things! But now they're comin'!"

Limping around to the front of the bar, Mr. Taney switched the lights on. The thick evening gold still wrapped around everything outside, but shadows were growing thicker in the bar. "You be careful now, Homer. They're in pretty high spirits. Some of them have already been drinking."

Homer grunted. "I can take care of myself."

The bartender frowned, "Like I said, be careful. Watch what you say. I don't want any trouble."

Homer moved to a spot at the middle of the bar counter. He liked to stand here when he could, right in the middle of things. Leaning back on his elbows he tried to look relaxed, but felt the tension in his stomach building.

"Are you going to buy anything tonight, Homer? Or are you just going to be a nuisance so that I have to throw you out again?" Mr. Taney asked.

Before Homer could reply, the small sounds outside melded into a babble of voices. Then heavy shoes clumped onto the porch and two field hands stepped through the door. "Hey, Taney! How about a shot of that watered-down whiskey you serve? You're gonna get caught some day, you know!"

The other hands pounded into the bar. "Come on, Taney, you old coot!"

Unable to stop himself, Homer shouted, "You guys act like you just come from a whorehouse!"

No one paid any attention. "We'll die of thirst if you don't hurry, Taney!"

Feeling a swell of desperation, Homer yanked the pint from his pocket and took a sip, splashing liquor over his chin when he was jostled. "Here, Homer! Don't waste that stuff!" Cable Johnston snatched the bottle away, tilted it into his mouth. Homer watched the man's Adam's apple pull the liquor down.

When the thick-shouldered bully just kept drinking Homer panicked, grabbed at the bottle. "Hey! That's enough! Don't drink it all!"

"You want it back?" Mr. Johnston thrust the bottle toward him, hitting Homer so hard in the chest that he flinched, "Here, take your whiskey back, fat boy!" He turned away. "Taney! For Christ sake!"

Grabbing Mr. Johnston's shirtsleeve, Homer whined, "Why'd you do that? You didn't have no cause to do that!"

"Get away from me, fat boy, go bother somebody else." Mr. Johnson shoved Homer again. "Anyway, you take up too much room."

"I was here first!"

"You hear that, fellows?" Mr. Johnston shouted, "Homer says he was here first!"

"Real good, Homer!" Jim Rosner lifted his beer glass in a toast, "That's the way to fight for your rights! Don't let that big ox push you around!"

"I said, move away!" Mr. Johnston shoved Homer so hard this time that he stumbled across the room.

"That's it, Homer!" Rosner began to laugh. "That's the way to take him apart!"

Mr. Johnson turned back to the bar, "Taney, give me another drink! I just defeated the fat-weight champion of Mooresville! I deserve a drink on the house!"

Homer crouched uncertainly until the men turned away, then crept slowly toward the bathroom at the far end of the room. Still facing the crowd he backed in, closed the door, and slid the latch carefully home before crumpling down on the toilet seat, covering his open mouth with both hands, squeezed his eyes shut. He felt like he might vomit, his stomach twisted tightly.

When he eventually began to regain control, Homer pulled his bandana out, scrubbed at the sweat on his face. Slowly, he heard the noise from the other room again. Shaking his head he said out loud, "It's no use." He should not have come to the bar. They only wanted to make fun of him. That was all they ever did.

Somebody knocked on the door, startling him.

"Homer, I got to pee!"

Not recognizing the voice, he stood up and stared uncertainly.

"I said, let me in! I got to go bad!"

"Go find yourself a tree!"

"Come out of there, Homer, or I'll kick this door down and drag you out!"

Snorts of laughter erupted in the background. Homer quickly opened the door and slinked forward, not looking at the person who brushed past. Stopping, he stared at the floor, sucking steadily on his lower lip, afraid to move any further into the room. The toilet flushed. When the man came out Homer finally looked up. It was Jim Jeffers, the only other person in the bar his age, though Jeffers looked younger because he was shorter. "It's all yours again, Homer. Sorry I disturbed you."

As he passed, Homer shoved Jeffers. The smaller man spun, clenched fists raised to shoulder level. Then he opened his hands and backed slowly away, "Easy there, Homer. I don't mean no harm. I just had to go real bad. No offense intended."

Homer stepped back into the bathroom, slid the latch home again.

Someone shouted, "Hey, what you doin' in there, boy? You gonna wear that thing out if you keep pulling on it! "

Unscrewing the top of the half-empty whiskey bottle the farm hand took another sip, trying to sift through the ragged confusion, trying to make sense of what was happening. The sharp slash of a blaring car horn cut through his thoughts. A swell of shouting rose from the men at the bar, "Well, I'll be damned! It's a bunch of women!"

Mr. Johnston's deep voice boomed out, "It's my cousin. I told her to come down. She said she would bring some friends along."

Sitting tensely, Homer listened to the excitement. He heard the higher pitch of female voices. Girls had come to the bar, girls out from the city! He had heard rumors about them coming down tonight. Wetting his bandana in the sink he ran it over his face, then tucked his shirt in, felt the small lump in his chest pocket. He had been waiting for this. Unbuttoning the metal button, he took a knotted rag out, carefully undid the knot and pressed the bills flat on his thigh one at a time to smooth them. He counted the bills, just to make sure. Twenty-three dollars, he counted them again slowly.

Then Homer folded the bills back into the rag, retied the knot, buttoned the rag back into his pocket and sat listening through the door, listening for female voices. He had practiced what he would say. He would get himself a city girl! Then he would have a story the men would want to hear, a story he could tell again and again. He would go out there and pick the prettiest girl, show her the money. Like Mr. Taney had told him, "They got to eat, Homer, just like the rest of us. That's where the likes of you and me get ours. We save up, see."

The boy had saved. He had done it only once before. The pocked-faced Towler girl used to take him into her barn to play "fiddle,", until her old man found them one day and nearly broke Homer's back with a hay rake. He had thought about all sorts of women sneaking out to his little apartment in the shed. But he thought mostly about the fine city girls; the kind the men were constantly talking about in the bar, the kind who "made the bottom drop out." And tonight, they were here.

Standing, Homer looked into the mirror, ran his fingers through his dirty brown hair trying to make it look better. He would go out there, look them over real confident like. Then he would stroll over to the prettiest one, maybe give her a pinch before showing her the money and leading her outside. Taking a last sip from the pint bottle to bolster his courage, he carefully screwed the top back on.

Nobody noticed Homer when he opened the bathroom door. The men swarmed around the girls, gliding restlessly through the faint shadows thrown by the soft lights. Standing silently at the end of the bar, the boy watched the others. One hand covered the lump in his chest pocket as he waited to be seen. The crippled bartender limped back and forth, serving beers.

After several minutes Jim Rosner glanced in his direction. "Hey, guys, look. Homer's finally let go of that thing and come out of his hole!"

"Homer!" Mr. Johnston said. "I would like you to meet my cousin, Wanda, come down from the city for a good time! Wanda, that there is Homer, fat-weight champion of Mooresville!" While the men laughed, Mr. Johnston whispered something into Wanda's ear. The girl, a pale, skinny little thing, smiled and waved. Homer tried to smile back, feeling his neck grow prickly with sweat as she walked toward him.

Lifting the rag out of his chest pocket, Homer worked to untie the knot. But his hands were shaking. He dropped the rag on the top of the bar, pulled feverishly at it, sucking loudly on his lower lip, until the corners fell apart, showing the dollar bills inside. Picking the bills up, the boy placed them on the bar-top, running his hand over them one at a time to straighten the creases and wrinkles.

"The boy's been busy!" Mr. Johnston said. "How long you been savin' up, son?"

Homer thought for a moment, "I don't remember."

Standing directly in front of him now, the girl gazed questioningly up into Homer's face. A corner had been cracked off her right upper front tooth. Homer tried to speak, but nothing came out. She stood a head shorter, her dyed blonde hair tied back with a pink ribbon. Wrinkles folded the corners of the large brown eyes in her narrow face. Homer realized she was older than he had thought. She just stood perfectly still, close enough to touch; the perfume she wore smelled like roses.

He couldn't remember any of the things he had planned to say. Homer grabbed the girl's right hand with his left, pressed the money into it. Then he stepped back and waited. Raising her hand slowly, the city girl counted the bills before looking quizzically back up at him. "Twenty-three dollars, what's this for? Why are you offering me this money, Homer?" Her voice rang out much louder than he had thought it would. Then she asked, "What kind of girl do you think I am, Homer?"

The laughter started again.

Homer stood staring up at the white specks of stars scattered across the black sky. Tonight was much colder; frost would come early. He looked again toward the dull glow of Mooresville as he sucked on his lower lip, chewing off a small piece of dried skin.

"She just laughed…I hope she starves!" He slammed his fists together. " She'll be starving and she'll come crawling back to me. And I'll just spit on her and walk away!"

But the excitement passed rapidly. They all hated him. No, worse than that, they didn't even hate him. They just didn't care. If they had shown some sort of feeling, if they had been really mad when they dragged him out the door and threw him off the porch, it wouldn't have been so terrible. But all they did was laugh at him, Mr. Johnston shouting, "Homer, kindly keep your fat, flabby paws off my cousin! She ain't that kind of woman!" before shoving him down again when he tried to get to his feet.

That was when Mr. Taney came out of the bar and made them stop.

Homer shook his head. He felt like he was living in a world where folks didn't even see him. No matter how hard he tried, no matter how loudly he shouted, no matter how many times he stamped his feet they kept walking right on by without noticing him. And he couldn't take it much longer. Homer searched through his pockets for his bandana, but it was gone. "Nobody could take it, the way they been treatin' me. Those lousy bastards, none of them's worth nothin', so they got to find somebody else to pick on. That's the truth!"

Stumbling on down the road, the boy tried to think of where he could get another drink. Mr. Schmidt, his boss, had a bottle of liquor hid in a shoebox under the parlor couch. Homer had seen him sipping from it one night while looking in the parlor window. The Schmidts would be in bed by now. Homer shook his head. But he wouldn't be able to get into the house without the dogs hearing, and the dogs didn't like him; they growed every time he came to the door.

"Or maybe if I went back into town, maybe they'd let me back into the bar…" Then Homer remembered that his twenty-three dollars were gone. Turning, he glared back toward the town, shook his fist. "I hope the bar burns to the ground and kills you all! I hope an earthquake happens!"

But the swell of anger felt empty, and he sighed, the sadness soaking through him. All he wanted was for the men to treat him the way they treated each other.

A soft light seeped from the partially open doors of Mr. Mason's barn. At first Homer did not notice the flickering of someone moving in front of a lantern. "Old man Mason's out there chasin' after the new hired gal. She went walkin' with Jim Jeffers yesterday afternoon. I seen 'em sneaking around together a couple of times. She's probably doin' it for him." Homer tried to picture the girl in his mind. "A little funny looking with that bent nose, but not bad."

Veering off the road, he stumbled through a potato field to the small window at the side of the barn. In the middle of the dirt floor sat Wanda, the girl Mr. Mason had brought in to help his wife. She sat facing him, trying to shield the light of the lantern from the large, open doors with her body and fondling something in the lap of her blue print dress. The girl's brown hair hung in braids over her shoulders and she had a soft smile on her face.

Creeping around to the front barn doors, Homer entered as quietly as he could.

The girl jumped up. "What are you doing here?"

Her voice was a low, irritating whine. He wondered what it had sounded like before her nose got broke? "Shhh. Want to wake everybody up? I was just walking by, saw the light. What you got there?"

"Go away, you're drunk. Get out or I'll call Mr. Mason!"

"I don't imagine Mr. Mason would be too pleased to learn that you been prowling around his hay barn in the middle of the night carrying a lantern." He stepped closer, "Come on, now. I'm just tryin' to be friendly. What you got there?"

"A kitten." Wanda looked down at her feet.

"A kitten."

"My kitten."

"Jim Jeffers give it to you?"

Wanda looked up.

"I seen you two together. But don't worry. I won't tell nobody." Squatting with a grunt, Homer began chewing on the end of a piece of straw. "I bet if Mr. Mason was to find out, though, he'd be plenty mad."

Wanda didn't say anything.

"Can I hold your kitten?"

"Why?"

"Why? Because I like kittens, that's all."

"No."

"No! What do you mean, no!" Homer wobbled, and almost fell over as he tried to stand up. Anger flooded through him. He stood ridged for a moment, staring at her, sucking on his lower lip. Then he slumped, wiped at the sweat on his forehead with his arm. "Look, all I want is to hold it for a little while. Please?"

Peeking up at him, Wanda lowered her head again, shook it almost imperceptibly back and forth. "No."

"If you don't let me hold it, I'll tell Mr. Mason I saw you doin' it with Jim Jeffers."

Startled, the girl glanced at him. Then she fidgeted uncertainly, hugging the kitten closer to her breast, her fingers pressing into it as it tried to get free. Finally, she extended the animal in both hands toward Homer, pulling back the first time he reached to take it. After a pause, she held it out again. This time she let go when he wrapped his large hands around it.

Homer fitted the small, all-black animal into the crook of his arm, stroked it. "I had a bunch of cats when I was a kid." He scratched behind the animal's ear. "Hello there, pretty little kitty." He looked from the kitten to Wanda. "You're mistress is pretty too, ain't she? Just like you, kitty." He stopped petting the animal, stared awkwardly at the girl as she stood with her head down. "I wonder why your mistress don't like me as much as she likes that short-stuff Jeffers, kitty? I sure could like her a lot."

Wanda didn't seem to hear. "Why's your shirt tore, Mr. Homer?"

"My shirt?"

"Your shirt, it's torn. Why's there blood on your arm?"

Grimacing, Homer tried to think of something that would sound good. "A bunch of the hands was picking on some kid. I helped him out."

"That was nice of you."

"I shouldn'a helped, though." Homer grunted, "People's got to learn to take care of themselves."

"Don't you like children, Mr. Homer?"

Ignoring here question, Homer asked, "How old are you?"

"Sixteen."

"Sixteen? By the time I was sixteen I had been working in the fields for four years. Ma threw me out when I was twelve. Said I was old enough to earn my own keep. 'Go find a job!' she said, 'and start payin' me back.' When she couldn't beat me no more cause I grew too big, she threw me out."

"Did you start paying her back?"

Homer looked down at the kitten as it began to purr. "Why should I? She lives just one county over, but she's never come to see me. I decided to travel back home once. She wouldn't let me in the house.."

"Doesn't she like you?"

Homer frowned, feeling his cheeks quivering, "She said I eat too much, that I'm stupid, that I smell."

"My ma don't like me much either. But she kept me around 'cause I could bring in money doing chores for the neighbors."

"Work is good for you. When I have kids, I'm going to make them start workin' soon as they can walk."

"You gonna get married, Mr. Homer?"

"What's the matter?" his gaze wandered nervously though the shadows of the barn. "You think nobody would have me? Yeah, I'm going to get married. And I'm gonna have kids, lots of them. And I won't throw them out. I'll give them a home where they can be safe!" The farmhand hit the left side of his head with his fist.

"You shouldn't do that, Mr. Homer." The girl reached out, almost touching him. "You shouldn't hit your head like that. You might hurt yourself." Wanda paused before continuing in a softer voice, "I like kids too. When I have mine I won't ever beat them."

Homer peered intently at her. It was hard for him to make out her expression in the low, shadowy light of the lantern, especially when she stared down at the hay-covered floor. But it had sounded so nice. Wanda finally raised her head, but immediately lowered it again when their eyes met. Even more softly she said, "Jim Jeffers likes kids, too."

"Yeah, I imagine he would say that." Homer spat on the doors. "A guy like him will say anything to get a little."

"No, he really does. He works on his uncle's farm. I've seen him playing with his younger nephews and nieces. He lets them climb all over him."

"Seems like you've been spendin' a lot of time with Jim Jeffers lately."

"Don't you like Jim Jeffers?"

Homer grunted, "He ain't much of a man, that's for sure. Don't even know how to fight. A woman should have a man who knows how to fight." Homer paused. His voice fell almost to a whisper, "Like me." Wanda stood fidgeting with a fold in the front of her dress. "You like me a little, don't you, Wanda? I ain't that bad, am I?"

"Jim Jeffers says he'll marry me as soon as he gets enough money saved up."

Homer grunted, began sucking hard on his lower lip. "No." he shook his head, "No, you don't like me. You're just like the others. You think I'm ugly and fat. Well, girl, you ain't so pretty yourself. How come your nose got bent that way?"

Wanda put her finger to the spot where her nose angled awkwardly to the left. "A man whose house my momma sent me to clean beat me."

"Didn't give him his money's worth?"

"Please give me my kitty back, Mr. Homer."

"Except for her nose, kitty, your master ain't so bad."

"Please give me my kitten back."

"You know, kitty, I'll bet she done it before, plenty of times, with plenty of different guys, not just the one who broke her nose." He winked down at the kitten.

As Wanda peered anxiously toward the barn doors, Homer took a deep breath. Then he almost whispered, "I surely would appreciate it if you'd give me a kiss."

Wanda did not answer. She looked at the kitten and then at the doors.

"Please, Wanda, don't you like me just a little?" Homer's hand shook as he reached out to touch her lightly on the arm. "I can work as hard as any man around here, and make lots of money. I'll buy you pretty clothes, and lots of kittens." His voice sagged into a pleading whine. "Please, Wanda." His voice faded completely.

After several minutes of limp silence, Homer hit his head again with his fist. Exhaling, he wiped his face on his shirtsleeve. When he spoke this time his voice had grown harsh, "Okay, what'll you give me for your kitten?"

Wanda's eyes went wide with fear. She raised her hands to her mouth, spoke though the fingers, "Please, Mr. Homer, I got to get back to the house. Please give me my kitten."

"I'll kill it. I'll kill your kitten if you don't give me a kiss."

Wanda started crying.

"All I need to do is squeeze a little, like this…"

"No!" Wanda grabbed for the animal. "Don't hurt it!"

He held her off until she stopped struggling and stood uncertainly before him. Moving forward, he backed the girl slowly toward an empty stall, "I won't hurt your kitten, or even tell Mr. Mason. All you got to do is give me one little kiss."

When Wanda tried to step around him Homer grabbed her with his free hand, shoved her down on the matted hay. As he stood above her she pleaded, "Please don't hurt me, Mr. Homer."

"I ain't gonna hurt you. I promise."

Shaking her head in disbelief, she repeated, "Don't do it, Mr. Homer. Please just let me go back into the house."

"Look, to show you how everything's gonna be all right, I'll put the kitten in this feed bucket. You can take it out after you kissed me." Meowing loudly, the animal dug its claws into the rim until the farm hand closed the flap.

Wanda tried to crawl out of the stall behind him on her hands and knees. Grabbing her, Homer dragged her back in.

"Stop it! Don't do that! I told you, everything's gonna be all right. Just don't get me mad!" Kneeling on the thin mat of dirty hay beside the cowering girl, he pinned her arms with a sweaty hug, pulled her in against him. "That's it. That's the way. My, you're soft and pretty. I'm not really all that bad now, am I? I'm as good as any of them other bucks."

The neck of Wanda's dress tore as he forced his hand down through it. "Please stop, Mr. Homer!"

"Shhh!" He glanced nervously toward the barn door, "I won't hurt you."

As he leaned her backward Wanda squirmed desperately, "Let me go, Mr. Homer! You're too big! Let me up or I'll scream!"

Homer sucked on his lip, "And get Mr. Mason out here? That old buzzard would beat you half to death for sneaking out at night. I'll tell him you been doing it with me. Then he'll send you back to wherever it was you come from. You want that?"

Wanda began breathing in whimpers as he forced her down on the hay. "Now just lay still. I'm not going to hurt you. Spread your legs a little, that's it." Wedging his knee between hers, he rolled over onto the girl as she struggled against him, crying loudly.

"Stop that noise, you want to wake people?" When she wouldn't stop, he clamped his left hand over her mouth, "Shut up! Did you hear me! Shut up!"

Wanda cried harder.

"If you don't stop cryin', I'll hit you! Do you want me to hit you?"

Gasping for air, the girl writhed franticly away from his body. "I told you to stop fighting! I tried to be nice! But you had to be just like the others. You had to try an' push me away." Wrapping both hands in her pigtails, he wedged her face between his fists so that she had to look straight up at him. A drop of sweat fell from his forehead into her left eye, causing her to blink. "Well, I got you now. I got you just where I want you. Nobody pushes me away! Do you hear?"

"Don't, Mr. Homer!"

Clamping his hand over her mouth again, he dug his fingers into her cheek. After several weakening attempts to twist her body away, Wanda stiffened suddenly; her face contorting. She choked, her head lurching upward. She shuddered and lay still.

When he was done, the farm hand stood up and buttoned his pants. Wanda slumped in the corner of the stall trying to cover herself with her torn dress.

"You hurt me, Mr. Homer."

"You done it before," he lifted his arm to wipe his face. "Don't try to tell me you ain't never done it before."

The kitten continued to meow, scratching at the insides of the feed bucket. While Homer slid his shoulder straps into place, the girl began to crawl slowly toward it, watching him carefully.

He smirked, "You want your kitten back?"

Wanda cowered., hugging her knees and chewing on one of her braids.

"Here. I'll give you your kitten back." Snatching the tiny animal from the bucket, Homer snapped its neck, tossing the limp body toward her. "All yours. And the next time I see Jim Jeffers, I'll tell him you ain't worth the effort."

Wanda remained crouched in the corner of the stall, staring down at the dead animal. She looked up at him, her face expressionless.

Grunting, Homer left through the barn door, shuffling slowly back out to the road. "Make fun of me, will they! Guess I showed them. Don't take nothin' from nobody! That's what my ma used to tell me. I don't need nobody to like me, specially some squash-nosed, stupid, little slut!"

He tried to laugh but the noise that came out sounded more like a hollow sob. Stopping, he wiped at his face again with his hand, "What's wrong with me? I just got me some." He walked on, "And once you do it with one of these girls, they keep coming back. That's what Mr. Johnston says."

After a second, desperate attempt to laugh Homer hit himself in the head with his fist. "Damn it! Why wasn't she nice?" He realized his left shoelace was untied. When he bent down to reach it, however, he almost fell over, had trouble regaining his balance. "I'm tired. I need to lie down." Nodding his head in agreement with himself, he moved on toward home. "I just need to get to bed."

Gradually, however, the farm hand's pace slowed until he stopped again, turning to stare at the barn. The faint light from the lantern still showed through the open doors. After standing quietly for several minutes, peering at the light, Homer groaned. Falling heavily to his knees, he beat at his head with both fists. "Damn it!

And I killed the kitten too!" Slowly he slumped forward until his forehead pressed into the macadam. He shook his head without lifting it, scraping his forehead on the rough surface. "I was gonna let it go. Only she got me mad, acting like I was doin' something bad. She was the one who made it happen." Straightening, he rocked back and forth until, suddenly, Homer jumped clumsily to his feet. Arms flailing out at the darkness, he screamed hoarsely at the softly moving, fields, "It was *them*! *They* made me do it!"

He melted into a cringing ball on his hands and knees in the middle of the road as he stared desperately back toward the soft light seeping from the barn.

When, finally the light went out, Homer felt like something had gone out inside of himself as well. Completely alone now, he began shivering uncontrollably in the darkness. It was so quiet. He just wanted somebody to talk with, somebody to watch, maybe even somebody to touch without them knowing it.

The only light still visible was the steady treetop glow from Mooresville. Straining his eyes toward it, he mumbled, "Maybe if I go back they'll have forgotten by now and let me back into the bar." He shook his head agreeing with himself. "I got me a real story to tell 'cause I did it tonight. They'll all want to hear about how I did it." He began crying. "Oh, God, they just got to let me back into the bar."

Stumbling to his feet, Homer hurried along the road back toward Mooresville. He tried to remember what had happened in the barn; he needed to tell the story right. He needed them to listen.

TAKING ACTION

Meghan Fort

Leaders preaching
Bloggers posting
Fanatics shouting
Crowds chanting
    Threats against the evil West.

Children joining
Boys learning
Men training
Insurgents acting
    For the Glory of Allah.

Ideas forming
Morals shifting
Minds bending
Senses numbing
    A new man is born.

Ready to follow the call.

Bodies lying
Infants crying
Debris drifting
    Because of one choice.

Civilians watching
Neighbors aiding
Soldiers fighting
Governments working
    To preserve liberty.

A Hidden World

Meghan Fort

Where I live
Faith in Allah is as
Plentiful as the desert sand
Beneath my feet.
Martyrs rise and fall
With the Arabian sun
Ready for a return
To purity.

This is a country of gods.
Gods whose influences reach
As far as the eye can see,
Snake charmers that mystify and
Entrance young men to bend to
The cause.

We live isolated.
Sheltered, they say, from the
Evils of the outside world.
We dispose of the corrupt and weak.
We are martyrs
Ready for the fight of our lives.

For Allah I walk in the fields.
I walk for the traditions of my fathers and
Burn in the heat of the
Violence I'm prepared to commit.
I am ready for my destiny.
I am a tool of faith.

The Witch of Endor

Andrea Robertson

The year everyone started to think the war was a bad idea, Sam Crabtree disappeared. Not run off, not moved by the DEA for informing, but actually disappeared, in that kind of way that nobody respectable had any solid idea as to his whereabouts. Just dissolved into the August haze.

"I heard he got mixed up with the Ogles," an Auxiliary woman would whisper, passing the flyer pinned outside the Valley Val-U Rite.

"S'what I heard. Nothing to be done for it. Nothin' at all," another would answer, just loud enough that it could be written off as an oversight of earshot, when his mother, Marilee Crabtree, heard them.

People talked, like they do, and people forgot, like they do, until a collage of missing dog posters, ads for Paul Gore's Tractor Emporium and flyers touting the Ingleside Ladies' Auxiliary club's annual charity brunch overlaid Sam's face. The weather made his youth run in inky rivulets right off the page. By late September, the former "REWARD: $5000!!! ANY INFORMATION ON SAM CRABTREE!!!!" read RE INFORM CRAB!!!", frayed at the edges, the same jaundiced yellow as the ribbons knotted around everybody's oak trees. Only one of the fringed tabs bearing Mrs. Marilee Crabtree's home phone was missing, torn off, stuck in the lining of Cass Bergeron's pocket, stinking like stale tobacco.

Cass Bergeron's man was missing too, but in a different kind of way than Sam. Cass had not heard from Jacob Mallory since March, when he'd sent a letter mostly of black blocks obscuring sensitive materials from an undisclosed location outside Baghdad, an arid tract of land heaven's eye was blind to. Cass didn't have a phone, so there wasn't that to worry about, which, in turn worried her more. The last letter was more black block than not, scribbled and spidery, just nigh of legible. Then they'd stopped, but no one had sent anything. There was no folded flag or anything, but Cass wasn't sure how common-law worked; she was pretty sure that it simply didn't work.

While there were plenty of theories explaining Sam's disappearance, only Cass speculated about Jacob's. There were all manner of threatening government acronyms that could be applied to it. But there was no body, no KIA to speak of -- AWOL or MIA, Cass didn't care for the sound of it.

Jacob had been deployed for around a year, back when the old folks in Zenith still thought he was going to fight for liberty, democracy and Christ off in the God-forsaken desert. Not that he was ever the military type—it just seemed at the time a better option than waiting out an Oxycontin charge in Bluewell Prison. But that was the summer before, when the high school still invited recruiters and Rayford Johnson still owned the Valley Val-U Rite. That summer was a long, long time ago. Or so it seemed. Left to her own, Cass noticed time passing both less and more, in spurts and jumps she didn't understand or try to.

Most days, she slept spread like a starfish on the queen size mattress that took up most of their shared bedroom, no longer regarding what was once Jacob's side of the bed. She'd wake in the late afternoon with the tang of her sleeping pill still in her mouth. With Jacob gone and her check from the State in the mail, there was only rare cause to leave the trailer. So it was rare that she did. Cass wore her confinement well, her usually bitten-bloody fingernails grown out, the pounds melting off her imperceptible under her summer shift dresses. Even her good teeth seemed more inclined to hang around with the house quiet and filled with only her presence.

While it can't be said the trailer was cheerful in particular, it was better than the bottom of the mountain. And for the most part, it wasn't all that lonely, either. Women kept coming to Cass, a pilgrimage among the army wives and mothers and sundry unfortunates who under different circumstances did their best to ignore her. None of them thought to ask if she'd found her own man yet.

It was neither surprise nor second sight that woke Cass on the morning of Marilee's arrival. Only crunching gravel. Marilee's car did not have the heft to make it up Endor Road, and the sound of gravel underfoot tied close enough to Jacob's arrest in Cass's subconscious to pull her into wakefulness. She'd expected Marilee for a while now. The news had dropped Sam's story, his name had slid to the middle of the Ingleside Methodist Prayer List printed in the back of the Watchman, a lower prayer priority now than rain. Cass scrubbed remnants of skin off last night's chicken bones, watching the church lady wend her way up the mountain.

"Good Lord." She sighed, but inflected like a question.

Cass's gift was the rarest. They say it's because the Lord is too good to put that mark on too many people. They say a lot of things.

There was another war going on, the year Cass was born, so lots of kids in the county were born just like her, with their fathers gone. For good. Now, hers wasn't dead, just disinterested, elsewhere, but it didn't seem to make much difference to the Lord, or whatever power marks folks with such things. There were other ones gifted, same age as Cass. The Boggess twins could stop blood and take thrush; that girl out Pickaway was a seer. They grew with their gifts the way a kid grows with anything, like leg braces or a crooked back or an ugly birthmark, making do. Most of them didn't practice, once they grew up, after they could control what amounted to a limp or a little hunchback in their lives.

But little Cass was the only finder. That was like being born with an aneurysm, or a hole in the heart. Fatal. Inescapable.

It didn't show. Not until she was older.

She found the Peters boy, just for his daddy to beat him to death a year later. Found a lot of people for the police, folks who'd have much rather stayed lost. She found the money Rayford Johnson's father buried, just so he could build that other house the snakes took over, and after all that, that crazy Rorrer woman killing him. It would be just the same, if no one ever mentioned again the staggering death toll of livestock and lost dogs she uncovered. Even her good bode bad. There was no contest against her clear sight.

"I've been expecting you," Cass said, before Marilee's raised fist hit the storm door. A grass stain clung to Marilee's left pant leg of her pink pant suit, her frosted hair made wild by the hike up War Ridge.

Cass leaned against the doorframe; her face turned away, a cigarette drooping from the corner of her mouth. She held a stack of Valley Val-U Rite fried chicken bones, denuded, polished and carved especially for the occasion in a red paisley handkerchief, one of the ones left behind by Jacob. Cass didn't read bones any more than she read the Bible; people love a good show. They need it.

Marilee lowered her head and smiled, tiny hands all gold rings, folded like a prayer.

"Yes. These are hard times. I'll bet you get a lot of women, looking for their boys, these days."

Cass shrugged. This was more or less true; her otherwise empty china hutch overstuffed with prescription bottles, most of which did not bear her name.

"I know you can't take money, because of the way it works…." Marilee whispered, cradling a skinny, midnight blue prescription bottle before passing it to Cass. "But I wanted to give you something."

Cass nodded, and placed the blue bottle in the hutch, behind the applesauce jar of Jacob's baby teeth. On some wild hair, Cass had painted the wood paneling a cheerful yellow, and since she didn't cook and ate little, the room stayed orderly enough.

"Not a bad little place you got here," Marilee said, following Cass into the kitchen. Her tone told tales—Cass knew other women must've warned Marilee to expect filth or squalor.

"Only just me, ain't so hard to keep on top of," Cass answered.

"Lord, I know it. No man in the house, no mess in the house." Marilee made a sound someplace between a laugh and a sigh. "I sure am sorry, about your man," She added.

Cass paused. None of her other clients had mentioned Jacob at all. She dismissed the gesture.

"You have something of Sam's? Something he used a lot? Or wore?" Cass pulled a chair up to her tiny kitchen table, nodding to Marilee to do the same.

"Yes," Marilee answered, dropping a silver lighter with a skull engraved on one side. She pressed her lips together, fighting against her embarrassment. "This is how I knew something was wrong, you know."

"How do you mean?" Cass asked, flicking it a few times to produce a weak flame.

"How I knew it wasn't just that Sam had run off and not told me. He did that a lot. But he wouldn't leave this."

Cass stared through the flame, distorting Marilee's image. Down at the bottom of the mountain, Marilee lived in a new house, one of the nice wood beam ones rich people paid Mennonites to build for them. Those houses, Cass figured, probably smelled like clean laundry even on days no one was doing laundry. Marilee went to church, she was Ladies Auxiliary Club, even. It would be possible, Cass thought, but difficult, for the two of them to be more different. But there Marilee sat, there Cass sat. What a world.

"You sound like one of 'em hippies over at Greenville," Jacob had said, his back to Cass, looking childish and alien with all his hair shaved off, smelling like work and young man. "I don't give two shits whether it's a good war or not, helluva lot better than Bluewell."

"You sure about that?" Cass sulked. The mattress was old and over-soft and welled up a little, a hill of cotton, polyester and feather between them. Jacob rolled over, pulled Cass over to face him.

"Yeah. Anything's better than Bluewell. I tell you what, war's war, but you don't get ass-raped in America's army. Man don't get raped t'all in America's army, s'got that much on Bluewell. And benefits beside. Get me some new teeth!" He grinned like a maniac. Cass laughed, but hid her face so Jacob couldn't see how quick her smile died.

"You see something?" Jacob had asked her, pushing a strand of hair off her face.

"It don't work like that, you know it don't."

"How does it work?"

Cass paused. In all the years of her finding, no one had asked her this. Maybe no one wanted to know.

"Hard to say," Cass grumbled, sure Jacob was trying to change the subject.

"Try to say," He answered.

She bit her lip, raised her hands as if she were pulling the answer from the air above her.

"It's like...like seein' the real end of stuff."

"The real end?" Jacob asked.

"Yeah, the real end. You see all these things that look like they could be ends, like someone movin' away, or somebody's animal runnin' off. But they're not all real ends. It's like a big tangle, you know? Of thread or somethin'."

"Thread or somethin'?"

"Can't explain better'n that," Cass said with resignation. "All I see is ends of things. Ain't even like seein', really. Feelin'. It's hard to explain."

"You high?" Jacob asked, laughing.

"Don't be a dick." Cass pushed him off of her. "I don't need to be a seer to know what you're doin' is goddamn stupid. Prison ain't so bad, lots of people go to prison. People get schooling in prison, even. Be good and you'll be out in no time. And hell, you probably got friends in there already."

"Why you so worried?" Jacob interrupted. "This thing will be over in, like, I don't know, a week, baby. Way before I even get outta boot camp." He rubbed her bad hip, with his broad hand. "They done caught Saddam, and after him then what else is there to fight for?" In the pale of the rising pink moon, Jacob was luminous and beautiful.

"And what if it does go on past your boot camp? Then what? Can't change your mind all of the sudden and be like 'Nope! I'd rather go to Bluewell!'" Cass wouldn't say it, she saw him thousands of ways. Feared him a thousand ways. A smeared paste of organs and camouflage, a saint George medal in the middle, eyes eaten out by vultures and skin blistered by sun even in death, a barefoot burqua slicing off his long hair, grown back in her memory, in a black plastic bag stacked with the rest.

"Be just fine. Never did much care for the humidity here, anyways. Bring you back some pretty scarves like the girl at the Val-u-Rite? Maybe a nice hookah, right baby?" He kissed her forehead. "I'll be back in no time, and the government's sendin' you money for me. Get the extended cable, huh babe?" His smile was the color of cigarettes, but had not yet fallen out.

There were such a few things more ludicrous than a backward mountain boy trying to make it in the desert, much less a desert city, in Cass's mind. Such a specific insanity, little baby men like Jacob walking unawares into a fray even the old men at the university didn't understand, without so much as a syllable of Arabic or Farsi in his head. The whole thing played at a crass joke.

The bed didn't creak so much as moan when as he pulled Cass into his arms, scrawny and green with scrawled, illegal tattoos. Jacob spoke in the low octaves of lovers, the subsonic rumbling of wiser beasts, like elephants or whales.

“Come on babe, we’re young yet. Fear is differ’nt than finding. Ain't the end of nothin'. There’s a long time to live yet for you and me.”

Cass dropped Sam’s lighter into a leather bag that held her phony oracle bones, hummed and shook it over her head, drooping, now, with the shame of her little joke.

“Where is he? Where is my boy?” Marilee pleaded.

Cass was reminded with no comfort of her first find, back during the war when she was a kid. Of her little-kid pudgy finger pressed on foreign coordinates, a hysterical fiancée recoiling in grief and disgust. How it wasn't Cass's fault, the weight of her mark on that woman, but it all amounted to the same in the end.

“Patience, madam. The oracle don’t respond to proddin’.”

Marilee watched Cass shake and shake the bag. Scam and con were harsh words for what she was doing—it wasn't as if she was full-on lying. She knew where Sam was. She'd been doing this for years, since before she dropped out of high school. Cass knew she shouldn't care about the sensitivities of some well-to-do church lady.

With a crash like cheap china against linoleum, she threw the bones onto the tabletop. Scrunching her itchy nose, face close enough to smell the southern-fried still sticking to the bones, she pretended to read them, studying like they’d advise her morality. Marilee followed their angles too. Cass was afraid her wide eyes were aware of the ruse, but the shine off them looked appreciative. “I see him.”

Marilee's eyes shined like a child's. She asked:

“Where?”

Cass had first seen Sam Crabtree three days prior to Marilee’s ascension into Endor, as she bought a bucket of chicken and a pack of menthols from the Arabs that Rayford Johnson had sold the Valley Val-U Rite to. Stopping in front of the poster where Sam smiled, frozen and fuzzy and happy in time, Cass raised her left hand to her head, trying to squeeze a headache out of her temples. Eyes cast at the floor; she spied the athletic sneakers of some church ladies in the back corner, by the bread stand, their whispers as low as their hemlines.

“Criminy,” Cass had said, and scrunched her eyelids like it would push the image out. The harder she worked, the worse it got, till she swore she could smell the body, even all the way down at the bottom of the New River.

"Poor girl, do you have headache?" The old Arab behind the counter asked, his lips pursed in sympathy. His daughter, her head wrapped neatly in a pink scarf, looked up from a paperback *The Things They Carried* with suspicion.

"Taking this, please ...." He extended a packet of Goody's powder across the counter. Cass winced.

The miles of murky water, the twisting road separating the Valley Val-U Rite and Sam Crabtree, what was left of him, pulled along the bottom of the river, pitted with caves and besieged by unfriendly currents bore the weight of Cass's clear sight.

He was mostly untouched, this early, the catfish hadn't noticed him yet, his blonde hair wafting around his blue, bloated face, his eyes closed fast and merciful. The hole James Ogle put in his back had stopped bleeding some fifteen miles downstream, and now, after the minnows'd had at it, was negligible. His Zenith Zephyrs sweat shirt billowed gracefully, the current tugging it down to his torn-out jean knees, feet bare and dusted blue. Sailing past the elaborate underwater canyons and small mountains of the bottom of the New River, Sam had never looked so beautiful. Cass's vision of him was a lot more beautiful than the photograph his mother had put up.

"Hey, Sahib, how long's that there been up?" she called to the Arab man behind the counter.

"Woman come in on Tuesday." He watched her suck the greasy air between her front teeth, pulling at the baby hairs up front of her scalp already graying. "Please, taking it, it hurts me to see such a pretty lady hurt like that." His daughter turned a page and muttered something irritable in Arabic, but he ignored her. He tapped the counter, crinkled eyes full of sympathy. "This woman, though, she is saying that her son is gone three months now, and police know nothing. It Is sad, you know? You know him?" The church women buzzed in the bread aisle like late August locusts. Out of the lot of them, Jolene Atwood's eyes burned on Cass's like they'd never pleaded her class ring and half a bottle of Xanax for finding the late Mr. Atwood. A whispery hiss wafting words like witch and cheat made them seem a genuine oversight of earshot. All the women held a hand over their mouths, two with rings and two without. Luck like Cass's was catching.

"Yeah. Sort of." Cass smiled, weak, slipping the packet from his fingers to hers, their fingers careful centimeters apart.

She tugged a fringe of Mrs. Crabtree's home number. Just in case.

But see now, here's the thing, the thing with the New River. People go on writing songs and poems and novels and all about the mighty Mississippi much as they damn well please, but no one bothers appeasing the New with poetry or power chords. Not only does she never give up her dead, she'll chew them till the oceans burn.

Pocked with deep holes, epochs-old throwback fish wait in caverns, passing straight on through to the other side of the earth. The river bed, the deepest part, is just waist deep in bones: bones of dead Indians, old French fur trappers, drunk settlers, drunk teenagers, over-confident fathers, murdered lovers, drug dealers, debtors, children; everyone thrown together, unsegregated, all sleeping in a disorganized, calciferous pile. What's lost didn't get found. There was no contest against the will of that river, the will of whoever put you down there.

Cass knew this. She knew that she could not be blamed for whatever she told Mrs. Crabtree, the New being the adversary it was. Cass could see Sam, resting, where the New meets the Gauley, becomes the Kanawha, upstate and over west by Ohio. Flesh peeling away from his bones, the catfish carrying his eyes and his hair waving like wispy water grass, he was still beautiful and peaceful even as the current exposed the framework of his fingers and face. The truth felt like Sam, heavy and rotten and gorgeous.

Cass gritted her teeth, impassive as the backmost molar broke.

Cass covered her eyes with a weary hand. She found herself regretting the dead clock on the wall, wishing for a noise—ticking, humming, anything—to break the tense silence that surrounded the two of them.

"Mrs. Crabtree, why are you here?" She asked, exhausted.

"To find my son," Marilee answered, her voice flat.

"Don't take no finder. And you ain't no fool."

The women sat in silence.

"Don't take no finder," Marilee repeated. "My sister was one, you know that?"

Cass shook her head. She'd never heard of another, and the thought of it made her a little sick to her stomach. Cass wanted to apologize for the bones, for the showmanship, but Marilee just laid her hands over Cass'.

"A hard thing to live with. Can't for very long."

"Hard to live like you are, too," Cass answered.

"Is there a body?" Marilee asked.

Cass sighed. "You'll never find it."

Marilee nodded. "The river."

"Yeah."

"Still moving?"

"Yeah."

"You see him, though? My sister always saw them," Marilee said. Seeing Cass hesitate, she squeezed her hands. "Tell me."

Cass breathed in:

"He's movin'. Slow. But over years and decades and eons what's left of him's keeping on. When he's just bone sludge, he'll be in the Kanawha, then the Ohio, onto the Mississippi...maybe the ocean? Maybe we'll drink him, or he'll rain on us. What's left of him'll last longer than us." The words belonged to Cass only by proxy—they moved through her like water.

Cass hated this part—the blame she felt anytime she found someone. There were finders who could track living people. She knew this. Cass was sure it was a moral failing, some deep-soul laziness that limited her sight. Some part of it had to be her fault. What cruel God would create a sight so useless?

Marilee who spoke first.

"Thank you," She whispered, "Thank you. Cass, you know the people he was runnin' with."

Cass shook her head.

"Only as much as anybody else." She nodded toward the hutch filled with prescription bottles. "Never needed them for my…habits."

Cass waited for the breakdown, for Marilee to scream or sob and pull at her hair. But she just stared at the bare chicken bones on the table in front of them.

"Well, you know of them. Since he started with them…feels like I lost him a long time ago. Like some of it was my fault. You hear women say that often?"

Cass sighed, rubbing her eyes. She felt a migraine growing.

"Not as often as you think. Look, Mrs. Crabtree, I'm sorry 'bout the bones and everything—sorry 'bout not bein' able to help you more."

Marilee waved her off. "No. It's enough. I just needed an end, you know? I'm ok. You know how when burns go too deep to be fixed, they don't hurt? Or when you get shot in a place they can't fix you, you can't feel it? There's not a thing to be done for it."

"Sounds familiar."

"Losing Sam. It's past hurting. Too deep for hurting. Nothing to be done for it.I just wanted an end."

Endings aren't so easy. Cass knew that, maybe better than anyone. You'd think, death was an end, but even that wasn't true—here she could still see Sam floating along the New River, here she closed out whatever image of Jacob that may exist. Marilee had hers, so she said. Nothing left to hurt.

Cass chewed one of the Oxycontin Marilee had given her. She could feel a vicious migraine coming on. The acrid powder tasted like strange hope. There was still pain. In the past eight months she'd swallowed a pharmacy and there was still pain. But pain could be healed, numbness could not. Cass felt tendrils of painkiller pulling her under, away from the throbbing behind her eye. There were worlds of pain left to feel. Cass smiled. She wasn't past saving, after all. Just in pain. Pain, she could live with.

Enhancement

Kimberly Meyer

Gun?
        Fifteen years.
Gang?
        Twenty years.
Third strike?
        Life.

Enhance my crime
so it looks worse.
Enhance my time
so I'm locked up.
Why not enhance my life,
so I don't do it again?

The Song of the Abyss Eater

Amos Wright

Still and all, when I was packed off to prison, not only was I innocent; I was naïve. Ten years later I got out, and everything was different from itself, but somehow itself nevertheless, and I was the most guilty man in the state. And this is a state with a bad conscience hanging over its head like a wall cloud that won't be blown away. I was guilty before prison, but not for what that kangaroo jury convicted me.

"This is a man who by the words of the victim herself repeatedly raped a little girl and we must therefore recommend the maximum sentence."

That prosecutor was slick as shit through a goose.

"You got to drive a white Bronco and then you can get away with murder."

My voice resounded like a silver light that grew wings and turned into a dove. When the dove perched somewhere, a dead tree downtown, they took a shot at it, and I fell silent. My bottomless gravelly baritone quieted, as in years past I ate socks in the corner which I came to study and know quite scientifically, banished there by my mother who was dismayed that I would not stop singing, could not just plain talk what I had on my mind, but forced it out in song and dance down the street. Now, with that prosecutor winking at the jury, the church choir would be sung without me into higher registers and the tenors and altos would have music space replying above the pews. All this attended by the angel Abaddon who I have arm-wrestled in jail.

The sorest part personally, is that I could've hitchhiked up to Nashville, singing *Mississippi Goddamn* or Erskine Hawkins, because they love a black man who can sing honkytonk or classical folk and bayou blues in Nashvegas. They clap for him and throw money at his feet. I must now be in a worse place to even commit these thoughts to words. Prison is where men go to face themselves. Bring on the greasy spoon reality in your limousine hearses. I have no more song to sing than a dirge.

At about the ninth hour, the courtroom was bustling like a bus stop back when gas prices soared. These tailgaters lined the wall and filed disorderly onto the plaza outside, like the aristocrats of old picnicking on the battlefield, watching the cannonball fly while stuffing themselves with caviar. They'd throw you out the front door of your own house, if there even was a door, so you can climb back in through the window and peekaboo, take a seat on the ratty couch and pretend nothing happened. I can't pass judgment upon creation by myself, can I? I might've made a killing selling tickets to my own trial, but they got laws against profiteering on your own suffering. Capitalize on your neighbor's suffering, they say.

Demeter didn't have the time to wait in line at City Hall before pawning the wedding band that once sparkled goldenly on her finger. Two years of work flipping burgers and do-you-want-fries-with-that cashed and collateralized for a shark loan. Demeter was gussied up for the show, my daughter Umbrosia nestling stoutly in her lap, bouncing on her knee.

The jury was white as a blank piece of paper on which you could write anything, whatever popped into your head. Not just folks who bubble in white on their income tax or the job application, but a bloodlessly pale species of specter modeled on scarecrows I used for target practice long ago. This jury is shit-scared of the boll weevil like the bogeyman. They know how to set the dinner table, where the forks and spoons go. Women whose cunts are dry as a popcorn-and-wine fart. Men who are now on the Highway Patrol. And not one of whom would look me straight in the eye and give me a yes or no.

What would you sell those tickets for? The courtroom was about out of oxygen. I hooked a finger in my starched collar and loosened up the tie my lawyer put around my neck like a goddamn noose. "You got to wear this if you want to impress the jury," he said, "Attaboy." He patted me on the shoulder when he was done like a high school gym teacher. Just on the off chance the jury had a sympathetic, color blind soul, or there was a nice looking lady in the audience you might want to ask out for coffee in ten years holding your breath the whole way. Sing the end. The end. All of Christendom was around the corner and up the block.

Sure, I had priors. Third-degree trespassing and driving with no license, but even Paul wasn't perfect. How's a man not supposed to trespass when they got the signs hung so high in a tree you can't even read it? Sheriff comes out, points at the orange no trespass sign up in the tree, says see that sign up there. No, sir I didn't. Oughtn't it to be at eye level? What if a trespasser can't read? You going to book an illiterate for trespass can't even read no trespass sign? Oughtn't you to book the superintendent of schools who gave this boy a G.E.D. when he can't even read a no trespass sign?

When they cut me loose, I had some things: clothes folded and crisply laundered, smelling of springtime soap, a letter from Judge Bahakel, some old keys that no longer unlocked any door, and a social worker's card that I tossed into the gutter among leaves and the unswept trash. Above the entrance were highfalutin words by some fool Cicero, *We are in bondage to the law in order that we might be free,* chiseled into the lintel above the courthouse door. I saw that folkshit soapbox the hindmost day of my freedom, before the one long night of my incarceration began. Out front is a statue of a condemned man. It might be sculpted from bronze or placenta, I don't know. In the distraught night, when the downtown streets drag alone, I think the condemned man sheds his shackles and takes a royal crap heavensent with wings on the lawn in front of City Hall.

The sky was pinked and loud as the strike of the gavel. I picked up a paper from the newsstand and read about my own release. I rolled the paper and tucked it into my pants and loitered in the plaza watching cars run the lights. I didn't know where to go or be. The highway behind the jail was taking people places in two directions. I could hitchhike, except for my thumbs.

Opposite the county jail, laughing white folks spilled out the front of the art museum and onto the sidewalk. Taking turns mooning over a waste of cinder blocks havocked into "art." I can peel the gum off my shoe and stick it on a tampon and call that art. Everybody clap for my song and dance.

I had some cash on me. I knocked around the 4th avenue north street, and watched a man take a shave inside a barber shop whose ribbon pole was busted and wouldn't turn red and white. They give you cash, saying don't spend it all in one place, and there maybe not one place to spend it. A man in a wheelchair grilling barbecue on an open pit in front of Green Acres.

I crossed 17th street and bought a ticket at the Carver Theater and sat in the back next to a woman or girl I couldn't see too good. Just snatches when the movie light flashed her way. She leaned into me and poured honey in my ear, ran her long-nailed fingers up my thigh and over my crotch. I paid this harlot for a ten dollar hand job in the dark as others went at it on the screen which had a rip in it. It had been ten years, cut a free man some slack. The brochures at the Civil Rights Museum don't tell you what the Carver is used for now. Old black Leonardo and peanut butter man sure sore about the grinding carnal relations and womanhood up against manhood transacted in his namesake. When I was that misadventured age I was pulling pranks like changing the street signs on the cops. No use improving a fool bent upon being foolish, what you might call the protection of the criminally innocent.

I turned south down 17th, night falling fast like a kidnapper pulled a black bag over the head of the city and dragged it off somewhere never to be found. The air around the Leer Tower was cooler and my skin burnished brimstone in the neon atmosphere of the night clubs that bumped wub wub wub music makes your ears bleed and give you soulburn. I love the gospel.

On First Avenue I squeezed by the tight sequined girls in high-heeled cork wedges, booties like two honey baked hams and all that ass hanging out of the miniskirts. In ten years, the skirts have gotten shorter and that is all I can report upon the nature of change. Each cheek glared at me like two nefarious thoughts. I snaked through the demimondes and shack-dwellers who slumped in doorways catcalling the bordello cockteases, many of them mothers as well as daughters once bathed by goner fathers.

I fell in behind a girl who could of been Umbrosia.

"Umbrosia," I said, grabbing the girl by the wrist and jerking her around.

"Get your hands off me you old faggot."

Women on your backs, when you close them eyes, think of Alabama. Do it for Alabama. It began to rain. I unrolled my newspaper and sheltered under it as torrents flooded my shoes. My photo bled ink in the rain. I continued the exodus out of downtown and into the west precincts where even the churches locked their doors.

Wife and child were on the porch like two properties taking a coffee break at the chattel quarters. I walked over my shadow down the long row of ancient shotguns. Umbrosia was no longer a child. She was with child herself. Looking about an ugly old eighteen. Sun in their eyes they couldn't see me too good. Then I called out in that voice they knew from church years back, the angry baritone that exalted the deity, and then they saw me by hearing me.

Umbrosia stood from the wicker chair with Zeniqua her half-sister, older now, who testified before all that I'd forced sodom and gomorrah with her. Rather to force myself on the back of the devil himself.

"You might ought to get on, Larson."

London's voice was like a creature scratching at the walls.

I stopped and the head of my shadow-self blackened the bottom step peeling white and flaky wood brown underneath.

"Just came to see my daughter. She ain't never visited me."

"She don't want to see you," Demeter said for Umbrosia.

"Never thought this day would come, did you?"

"You fucked them babies. I don't care what no judge rule," she spat at me.

I stepped back. London came out of the summer darkness of the house and began loading red shells into the breach of a shotgun that used to belong to me. He looked bloated, big as a tick.

"Shit, London. You can't shoot a man with his own gun. How many you had today already? You ought to put that away, if you can shoot straight. Why don't you step back inside and take another lick from the juice bottle?"

"You still got that smart mouth, ain'tcha?"

"Not smart enough not to spend ten years in jail," I said, extending in covenant my right hand for London to shake. I never got that hand back. Of course, London had been there that day in the courtroom to say before all that would listen, "If you don't convict this man of the awfulest crime between members of their own family, I'll spill his guts myself."

"Thank you, London." They were listening.

A child rapist is lower than a motherfucker in prison. Hardened criminals got a pecking order to inspire superior feeling. I'd have been better off if I'd killed the girl after I was supposed to have raped her. As if the fact of her wandering still torn through the civil world was reminder that many had thought about heinousness, but only a few were both righteous and wicked enough for the deed.

I buckled down. I got my G.E.D. I heard the word recidivism

used by a social worker and got down the dictionary and looked it up. I slept close to a copy of Malcolm X's autobiography given to me by the appellate lawyer who used a lot of fancy lawyerly mumbo-jumbo. Words like reducto absurdum and audi alteram partem. Hauled away in handcuffs before the tearless eyes of Demeter and our daughter, I hollered and cussed the jurors using archaic words not used since the last century, in a voice from which gospel had once praised all creation between heaven and its opposite.

Most nights after work, I bathed Umbrosia and her half-sister Zeniqua and listened to the TV on in the backroom. I washed lice out of Zeniqua's hair and washed carefully around bruises. Sometimes I sat on the toilet with the lid down reading the paper as they splashed in the bathtub. Their mother caroused home when she remembered where home was. That night, I'd promised to take care of the girls, little as I liked to promise anything. When I was younger I'd hustled through women. Now, I stayed at home, like I couldn't get a date to the dance.

I heard London barrel through the front door and into the living room. You always hear a man like that before you see him. "Where's your sister?" he asked Umbrosia in his voice destroyed by smoking and screaming and drinking. We'd once stood shoulder to shoulder together in the choir, he an atheist who intoned songs of hope and afterlife. But he took to that godless outlook and he got angrier and became a late night arguer and more spavined in the head. He got mixed up with Demeter before I got remixed with her, foresight being more survival than hindsight. The man can't keep his ears clean now without a woman around. I think he is barely employed and might not even be able to hold his own cock. Nor would I leave him in charge of a single houseplant on the kitchen table. See after all those seasons of cropping the cotton we still as a people have no green thumb. Our thumbs got amputated in the machines of dicksquat. So I am *father* to *his* accident with *my* Demeter. But I out-suffer, etc. I don't think he's ever suffered a hangover either, because he never bothers to sober up.

I couldn't hear Umbrosia's answer, and London probably didn't either. Umbrosia had the soul of her mother – anarchy. I'd met her mother sponging at the car wash, bending over the hood in blue jean cutoffs, her black Miss Alabama's ass peeking out like a scalding hot liquid poured onto your lap in the shape of a Venusian woman. Shit and goddamn, Demeter was a black black woman. We had some good times together. Happiness is always a recreated thing way back when, never the pot of food sitting before you on the table. The food might taste like nothing, but it always gets better.

I was toweling down his daughter when London weaved into the bathroom. I could smell the bar on him. I remember the towel, its downy texture. It was a white towel Demeter often used by the pool, and imbrued splotchily with an oval stain from blood or coffee. I don't know what London thought he saw, or what he thinks he remembered, but I'll be goddamned if I wasn't more a father to Zeniqua than he was, even if I touched that girl.

I worked the fryer at Burger King then moved up to McDonald's. A decade later, Leon was still working the drive-through window.

"You ain't retired yet?" I wheedled him.

"What's up, Larson? Heard you got a wrongful conviction."

"The little bitch revoked her testimony."

"Ain't that a blessing."

"After everything I done for her?"

"That was a long time ago."

"Can you help a fellow out? I need my old job back."

"I don't know, man. You'll have to come back. Maybe the manager can find something for you on Monday."

"I can clean the windows," I said, pointing to a pink ice cream stain dripping down the face of the glass.

"Not sure we need any help right now."

"Remember that time you screwed that girl and found out later she was a he. What was her name? Donald?"

"How can I forget when you won't let me?"

"And then you find out, get this, his first name is Mac."

"That was a long time ago."

"He was one fine piece of ass, though."

"There's a customer waiting behind you," Leon said leaning out the order window, a customer's irate voice squawking into his headset.

"Hold on a fucking minute," I said to the car inching its front bumper up to me.

"I'll have one of them hot McApple McPies, McPlease."

Me and my McApple pie sorrowed over to Oak Hill Cemetery. A pretty picture of an ugly reality: the northside view of the big bad city, this babylon dying slowly of buses and mayors and weeds. I saddled the ironwork fence that segregated the buried dead from the living in their cars and office buildings. A water tower on the hill above threw a plumbeous shadow across the cemetery lawn. Each of the FBI building's dark windows, an opportunity to confess.

The cemetery was trashed and disrespected. Among the living, reverence for the dead is basically at a low point never before seen. Old dentist chairs dumped by a crumbling mausoleum. I took a seat in one of the vinyl chairs and leaned back, opening my mouth so my carious molars got a peek at the sky for the first time. A passenger airline banked east overhead. The dental chair squeaked forward and from my throne I surveyed the headstones furred over with mosses and the lost names worn by rain. There were moments of green, freshly planted grass over the newest dead, and white marble crosses christless and lichened, and polished pink granite tombstones that reflected the living in their passing among the graves. A bird nest tucked away in the arm of one giant cross and the eggs fallen to the ground, broken, unhatched.

Mourners gathered under a tent. I saw them first reflected in the gleam of a big hearse parked under a black oak: the crowd carrying candles across 11th avenue north, singing of the resurrection of the body, then passing through the gate and dispersed among headstones. I was wondering whose grandmother had died for the second time, any excuse to get out of school, when I got a peek through the hunched shoulders of the mourners at the named carved into granite: Shuttlesworth.

Prison is where men go to face themselves in the company of other men's solitudes. You don't know who the fuck you are, do you?

I crossed under the interstate again and came up behind a black car parked beneath the overpass. Windowless with the state license plate ripped off. It smelled like a barbecue gone bad. The upholstery was burnt up and the dashboard plastic curled and bubbled. I pulled my shirt up over my nose and peered in through the glassless window. A man and a woman still inside. Botched burning where here and there flesh clung cured but sure to the bone.

A hipshot out-fangled woman was rolled up to the glass in a wheelchair, a brightly knitted afghan thrown over the sticks of her legs. Mamma looked older, aged since the trial. She'd been sniveling already. "You don't got to say nothing, Mamma," another I said inside me. Mamma was the toughest woman I knew and it broke me up to see her broke up. She reached her liver-spotted claw across the table and the fingers uncurled like the legs of a dead spider. Restrained by handcuffs, I couldn't take her hand.

"My baby," she bawled.

The other inmates turned to stare quietly.

"Everything alright here, mam?" a guard asked.

"I'm fine. Fine. Excuse me."

When the guard returned to minding his own fucking prison business, "How about Demeter? When she going to come see me? I been in here six months already and I ain't heard nothing from her. Not even a perfumed letter."

"I think it best if she just forget about you. Her and Umbrosia. You can't be no father to that baby girl behind bars."

"Once a bitch always a bitch."

"She got some papers here she want you to sign, Larson."

Mamma pulled a square manila envelope out of her handbag and slid it across the table to me. "I ain't sign shit. I got a lawyer says I don't have to sign nothing."

"I did my best to see you was raised up right. You had the best voice in the choir. What'd you go and break us hearts for, Larson? What for?"

Back in my cell, I tore up the papers into confetti and turned over everything else inside of my nine-by-eight suicide watch. At night, I sang my fellow abyss eaters to sleep and perhaps to dream that the world is good, even on their side. My voice walked through the iron bars and reached like a hand into their hearts and crowned us brothers heads bowed not in prayer but under the weight of agonistic legal fictions evaporated into thin airs.

Man digs himself into a hole, meanwhile looking only at the sky. Woman points out that Man is in a hole. Man tries to dig himself out of the hole and the hole deepens. Let's face it, some holes aren't holes at all. They're abysses. And all you can do is try to sing and eat the abyss at the same time. All that matters is your capacity for the out-suffering of others. Just give the abyss a hug, squeeze it like a child; the child you raised up right from wrong.

I went back, way back to Beulah Baptist where I got churched-in, metaphysical bullshit, my soul brined in the pickle jar of the Gospel of John according to John. In my boyish irreverence, around the time my voice started cracking and hair budded in funny places, every Sunday morning it was the same worriment: my cock was unhappy in my left pant leg, and how do I get it slung over to the right pant leg before we all stand up singing hallelujah and I with my Sunday best pants proud as a popped tent. Those wool dress pants were tight and hot, we couldn't afford more than the one pair and you had to wear them till the seat fell out and the knees were worn from so much kneeling prayer.

The heavy wooden door was open. I pushed through and into the dim vestibule, where I'd shook hands many times with the minister after service. The pews empty row after row. This very voice, in a purple choral robe, that is now loquacious in your head once soliloquized the sob story of the Christ child and the Jewish kids scared of Herod. I pulled a hymnal from the back of the pew in front of me and it creaked open to torn out pages. You see, if we ain't got no thumbs, we can't hitch nowhere.

The door of the rental office chimed as I walked in and sank into a plush carpet about six feet deep. A brindled office man in a madras shirt was slowly dying behind a desk covered in papers. A stuffed owl with bright yellow eyes watched us from the wall.

"Can I help you?"

"Looking for a place."

"You come to the right place for a place. You'll just need to fill out an application, and our office will run a background check."

"I can tell you right now what the background check's going to be."

"Maybe you come to the wrong place, then."

"I didn't do it."

"What'd you not do?"

"Don't matter. I got cleared."

"Still, we'll need to a run a background on you."

"Cleared means I didn't do it. I'm in the church choir."

"I understand, but there are procedures."

“Look here, I got a letter from Judge Bahakel hisself says I didn’t do shit and I go to that Judge and say you won’t rent, he’ll hand you your ass on a fucking silver platter like John the Baptist’s head.”

“That’s some language for a choral man. I’ll have to think about it. We got children in our buildings. What are mothers going to think they find out who’s living next door?”

The letter from Judge Bahakel under his nose put the heat on him.

“I got a vacant house on Cotton you can fix up.”

“I’ll pay you soon as I get a job. Be making McMinimum wage.”

“Making McWhat?”

I could see his face in a frying pan.

“Nothing.”

“One slip up and your ass is on the street.”

“Mighty kind of you.”

I found the apartment unfurnished and unwatered on Cotton Avenue. The front porch held together with C-clamps and jerry-rigged four-by-four posts. Saplings sprouting out of the gutters choked-holded with leaf rot and dead birds. I fit the key into the door, which wasn’t even locked, and the hollow board door swung open on whining hinges into an empty, pitchy room. With my foot I swiped cockroaches onto their backs, skidding them huskily into a corner. I put my hand to a grey waterstain bubbling the dry-wall ceiling, still damp and cool to the touch. Some animal had left artifacts of its tenancy behind. I flipped a wall switch. Nothing works the way it’s supposed to around here. In the kitchenette, the windows were without blinds if there was even glass and everything let right on in, help yourself. A dark inkling of yellow streetlight trespassed into the room at nightfall. The only water in the dump was inside the back of the john.

I went out the next day to raccoon through street garbage. Back of an old furniture store I picked up a chair and a wall clock with no batteries. I placed the chair against a wall and watched a trapezoidal door of sunlight slide across the hardwoods and climb up the east wall like a creeping exit. The walls clanged and rattled as water coughed up the pipes.

I got up and went to the bathroom and sat on the roll rim of the cast-iron claw foot. A thread of rusty coldwater untangled out of the spigot and pooled in the basin before it swirled down the drain. I plugged the drain and took off my clothes like they make you do when processing you between worlds, out of the crowded wasteland and into the solitary wilderness. The clothes I changed into upon my eviction back into the free world lay in a puddle on the tile floor.

I slid in up to my neck in steaming water. First time I'd even seen a tub like this since I'd washed my own daughter and her half-sister. Above the tub was a window grayed with soot and a little view of a true sparrow warbling to a white pigeon. What little leaves were hanging on were changing. It would be time to Fall Back soon. I'd never kept track of time in prison. No calendar to turn every month, with the days of perfectly black boxes to slash through. Ten years the same as one long day, the sun's rising light just good enough to bless the night before it comes.

I wiggled my toes underwater and snorted in a breath. My mouth opened and a gospeler's verse unheard in a long time echoed throughout that empty apartment a thousand times stronger than the judge's walnut gavel banging on the bench when I was thinking: I'll rape all ya'll's women, so when they come back for me, they'll have a real good reason this time and the law says you can't try me twice for the same crime. I cupped my hands and splashed water over my face. Goddamn if a sequined, honey baked ham wouldn't be deluxe right now. My old voice came back and furnished the rooms with purple-robed people descanting the melodies of hymnists. They multiplied and crowded together singing until someone was beating on the door, begging me to shut up, like the cops had beat on the door the night I was bondaged. And because when I sing, my voice exists for a time outside me, I am not alone.

I'll never stop with the melancholy hollering singing hosannas and miserers. For even in prison I had my singing voice, the only person that never left me. I call it the song of the abyss eater. I'll sing it for you, up to my neck in bathwater. It goes like this.

SUBHUMAN

Meghan Fort

Heat slams against the cold bare ground.
Thick soles scrape the floor and stop.
Stale sandy air swirls above
As a faint reminder of freedom outside...
If one could call a desert paradise.
Above, an angel speaks to me - forcefully.
Words, moans, cries of anguish blend
Together into a song fitting of this place.
A tug on the rope and back to reality.
I am an animal.
I am a terrorist.
I am whatever you desire me to be.
As my body bends in submission to each pull and burn,
So does my will.
Fear yields to terror.
Anguish morphs to despair.
Hell on Earth has arrived.
I am ready to throw my mangled body to the wind.

THE CRYING WALL

Short Story by Victor Hassine, Adapted for the Stage

Adi Stein

The set consists of three prison cells upstage on a raised platform. They look like boxes with classic prison cell bars as doors. There is a platform with railings in front of the cells. Downstage of the center cell is a set of stairs which lead downstage to a bare floor. Stage right of this floor is an enormous, tall white wall. The wall looks like it shoots up into the heavens and further.

Lights up.

In the center cell is Young Man. He is around 20 years old. He looks young. He looks around as various inmates walk across the platform in front of him, studying their every movement.

Buzzer.

The cell doors open and the two men in the cells on both sides of him exit. Every other inmate is gone. The two men just keep walking back and forth across the platform in robotic motions.

Enter Old Man. He is 73 years old. He moves at a slow, deliberate pace. He is short but carries himself well. He walks in holding a steel bucket filled to the brim with water and a white washcloth. As soon as he enters, Young Man is fixated by him.

Old man dips his washcloth into the bucket and begins to wash the wall. As he washes it, Young Man begins to make his way down the stairs, studying Old Man. He is standing at the middle of the stairs. Throughout the following dialogue, Old Man continues to wash the wall as if no one was talking to him.

YOUNG MAN
Hey! Whatcha doin'?

Silence.

YOUNG MAN
Hey! Old man! Whatcha doin'?

Silence. Young man begins to make his way down the stairs.

YOUNG MAN
Old man! I'm talking to you. What are you doin'?

Silence. By this point Young Man has reached Old Man.

YOUNG MAN
Old man, you best not ignore me again.

Silence.

YOUNG MAN
Did you hear me? I said you best not ignore me again!

Silence.

YOUNG MAN
What are you, deaf?

Young Man gets between Old Man and the wall.

YOUNG MAN
Look here, old timer. I wanna know what you're doin'. Why are you washing this fuckin' wall?

OLD MAN
Move.

YOUNG MAN
Not until you explain this to me.

OLD MAN
Move now.

YOUNG MAN
No.

OLD MAN
Now.

YOUNG MAN
Man, fuck you.

Old Man slaps Young Man across the face. Young Man freezes in shock, eyes wide.

OLD MAN
You have no respect. Absolutely no respect. Do you have any idea what this wall has been through? Do you have any idea what this wall has seen? It has seen more than you could ever know, yet you stand here and ignore it, trying to disrupt my care. Come with me.

YOUNG MAN
Fuck no! You just fuckin' slapped me!

OLD MAN
(in a commanding tone)
Come with me now, young fool.

For whatever reason, Young Man listens. They walk center stage and stop. Old Man Points to the base of the wall. A large dark spot has formed at the base.

OLD MAN
Do you see that spot?

YOUNG MAN
Yeah, what about it?

OLD MAN
That is the stain that has grown and grown over time from the tears of this suffering creature.

YOUNG MAN
What? Are you out of your mind? It's a fuckin' water stain from the motherfuckin' rain. What the fuck are you on?

OLD MAN
It is the collective tears of a wall that has existed and will exist forever, watching atrocity after atrocity.

YOUNG MAN
You are out of your mind.

Old Man points to a section of the wall about three feet off the ground.

OLD MAN
Do you see that stain?

YOUNG MAN
What stain?

OLD MAN
That is where a young man, about your age, was stabbed for absolutely no reason.

As the following examples are demonstrated, Young Man gets progressively more restless and shakes with anger and confusion.
Enter two inmates, one small and young, the other large and older. They stand about a foot from the wall. The older one takes out a makeshift knife and plunges it into the young one. As he does this, a red stain appears where Old Man was pointing. The young inmate remains dead on the ground as the old one walks offstage.

OLD MAN
And that crack in the wall *(points to a section of the wall about 2 feet above where the red stain is)* is where another man died.

An inmate walks in. He paces back and forth. He slams his fist on the wall. Slams it again. He slams his head into the wall leaving a crack. He slams it again and again and again and again until he collapses, dead.

OLD MAN
Or all of those bullet holes.

Old Man draws a line through the wall about 4 feet up from the ground with his fingers. As he does so, three inmates run in, trying pointlessly to climb the wall. There is a loud sound of automatic weapon fire that comes from dozens of feet over the heads of Young Man and Old Man. The inmates collapse one at a time, one atop the other, dead, as the bullet holes show up exactly where Old Man said. Young Man is totally devastated by this point.

OLD MAN
Do you see now? Do you see what this wall has seen? Do you see the death and destruction that happens here? This is not a prison. This is not a holding facility. This is a death camp. We are all doomed to die here, and this wall will see it all. It will certainly see the death of you, young fool.

YOUNG MAN
(with a total loss of control)
No! No! You are crazy! I will not die here! I will not die like them! You are crazy! You see this fuckin' made up shit and try to convince me it's real? Fuck you! Fuck this place! Fuck this wall! YOU ARE OUT OF YOUR FUCKIN' MIND!

Young Man runs back up the stairs into his cell. He sits on his bed, holding his head, crying.

Old Man Walks up the wall, no longer white but now covered in marks and stains, and stands among the dead. He dips his washcloth into the bucket and slowly approaches the wall with it. As soon as he makes contact, a stream of water falls down the wall, covering the stage.

Fin.

The Ones I'll Leave Behind

Jordyn Cahill

Within these iron bars are years of female rage
Bound by pasts so discolored, they now cry within this cage.
Tears shed for children lost,
Of men they knew before,
Sobs echoing off concrete halls from screams that they were whores.
Panic fills the darkened void as they try desperately to forget
The taste of life bitter upon their tongues from digesting their regret.
Some come and leave and act as though this is any other day,
Some are discarded by society and embraced by shades of grey.
They adapt ways of madness
Conform to what they think will cure
The aching in the pits of them
The bloodied and the pure.
The darkness is binding and light is rarely seen,
Music comes from silence and the never-ending screams.
Guidance is fed by thugs, and the occasional angel from above
Each of us dehydrated from the lack of someone's love.
For many moons uncounted, I have watched these women live,
This ordeal has taken pieces of me that I never chose to give.
I know my end is coming,
The day will soon be mine,
But still my heart is aching for the ones I'll leave behind.

About the Editors and Contributors

ZOÉ ORFANOS (Editor-in-Chief) is an undergraduate student at American University in the School of Public Affairs. She graduated High School with both an International Baccalaureate and Honors diploma and is currently working toward a Bachelor's degree in Law and Society with minors in Creative Writing and Literature. Orfanos recently achieved the Best Poem for the most recent edition of BleakHouse Review.

ROBERT JOHNSON (Consulting Editor) is a professor of Justice, Law, and Society at American University and a widely published author of fiction and nonfiction dealing with crime and punishment. His short story, "The Practice of Killing," won the Wild Violet Fiction Contest in 2003. His best known work of social science, *Death Work: A Study of the Modern Execution Process*, won the Outstanding Book Award of the Academy of Criminal Justice Sciences.

FELICIA AFUAN (Associate Editor) is a sophomore honors student studying Law & Society and Philosophy at American University. She is originally from Northern California and has interests that span many disciplines, including writing, photography, and understanding the justice system.

HANALEAH HOBERMAN (Associate Editor) is an undergraduate student at American University in the College of Arts and Sciences. She is currently working towards a bachelors of arts is psychology with a minor in creative writing. Hoberman has published articles in local community newspapers in Austin Texas and in the Eagle, American University's student newspaper. Most recently, she was recently admitted to the Phi Beta Kappa national honors society and won the Mathias Award for Undergraduate Research.

LIZ CALKA (Cover Design) is an award-winning photographer and undergraduate student at American University majoring in Visual Media and minoring in Graphic Design. She serves as Artistic Director of BleakHouse Publishing. She has created covers for multiple BleakHouse publications in addition to *Tacenda* including books *Origami Heart* and *A Zoo Near You*, and *BleakHouse Review*. She also created and maintains the BleakHouse Publishing website.

CARLA MAVADDAT (Cover Design) is the Assistant Art Director and Curator for BleakHouse Publishing, an award winning photographer, and an undergraduate majoring in Political Science at McGill University. Mavaddat has a passion for photography and design, along with a longstanding interest in human rights and social justice. Her creative work has appeared in several venues, include *Adore Noir*. Mavaddat has served as Editor for the 2011 and 2012 issues of the online literary magazine, *BleakHouse Review*, which features a distinctive noir aesthetic.

SONIA TABRIZ (Text Design) is a merit scholar and J.D. candidate at The George Washington University Law School, where she is Editor-In-Chief of the *Public Contract Law Journal*. Tabriz graduated with honors and *summa cum laude* from American University with majors in both Law & Society and Psychology. She received the Outstanding Scholarship at the Undergraduate Level award from American University for her award-winning works of fiction, legal commentaries, artwork, presentations, university-wide accolades, and academic achievement. Tabriz is the Managing Editor of BleakHouse Publishing.

JUSTIN SONG (Text Design) is a senior at American University pursuing a Bachelor's Degree in Law and Society and Philosophy. His interest in law sparked through his experience interning at various DC-based humanitarian non-government organizations and through his studies at the London School of Economics. He is originally from Ithaca, New York and hopes to one day attend law school in order to teach legal theory, though he is open and curious of anything he may discover on the way there.

MICHAEL E. BALLARD (Author) is a prisoner on death row in Pennsylvania whose talents include creative writing and art.

JORDYN CAHILL (Author) is a prisoner at Gadsden Correctional Facility with a passion for creative writing and plans to work as a writer upon her release.

MEGHAN FORT (Author) is from Charleston, South Carolina and currently a junior at American University majoring in International Studies.

CARLA MAVADDAT (Author) is an undergraduate majoring in economics at McGill University with a passion for photography and design. She is originally from Montreal, Canada, but grew up in Washington, DC. Carla is interested in human rights, in social justice, and is a strong advocate against poverty. She served as Guest Editor and Designer for the 2011 issue of *BleakHouse Review*.

KIMBERLY S. MEYER (Author) is a recent graduate of American University's Master of Public Administration program, where she concentrated in social justice policy and served as Editor-in-Chief of the school's peer-reviewed academic journal. She currently works as a Research Associate for the National Council for Public-Private Partnerships. With hopes of pursuing future doctoral studies and publication in the field, Meyer's research interests include juvenile sentencing, capital sentencing, and the provision of human rights in the criminal justice system.

ANDREA ROBERTSON (Author) is a recent graduate of American University of Washington D.C.'s MFA Creative Writing program. My work has previously appeared in Ghost Town and Panhandler magazines.

WILLIAM ROTH (Author) is currently a professor at Kutztown University. Two of his short stories have placed in national competitions – Serpentinia and New Millenium Writing. He has also published stories in The McGuffin, The Schuykill Valley Journal, Overtime, and Tacenda Literary Magazine. His first novel, "The Pelican the Pearl and the Live Oak Tree," came out this spring.

ADI STEIN (Author) is a recent graduate of American University with a degree in Theatre: Performance and in Philosophy. Toward the end of his AU career, Stein began writing and instantly fell in love with it. Having written several 10 minute plays, a few one acts, and two full length plays, two of his 10 minute plays have been produced by local DC theatre companies (Security was produced by AU Players and Snap was produced by The Apron

Theater Company). In the coming months Stein will direct Jesus le Momo in the Capital Fringe Festival, and following that I will appear in Body Awareness, the first show of Theater J's 2012-2013 season.

AMOS JASPER WRIGHT (Author) is a native of Birmingham, Alabama. After two years drifting hand-to-mouth in Boston, he returned to Birmingham and recently completed a master's in English at the University of Alabama, Birmingham. Upon realization that he must work for a living, and after acquiring experience in architecture and planning, he applied and was accepted to Tufts University, where he will enroll in the fall of 2011 to begin a master's degree in urban planning. He has high hopes that two master's degrees will equal a PhD. His fiction and poems have appeared or are forthcoming in New Ohio Review, Salamander, Pale Horse Review, Arcadia, Union Station Magazine, Zouch and Yes, Poetry. He is also co-editor of the White Whale Review, an electronic literary journal, and The Heaviest Corner, a blog devoted to urbanist issues in Birmingham.

www.ingramcontent.com/pod-product-compliance
Lightning Source LLC
Chambersburg PA
CBHW070649120726
47909CB00004B/1643

* 9 7 8 0 9 8 3 7 7 6 9 2 5 *